EASY PIANO

THE GIANT BOOK OF
CHRISTIAN MUSIC

MW00824100

Arranged by
CAROL TORNQUIST

ALFRED

Produced by
Alfred Music
P.O. Box 10003
Van Nuys, CA 91410-0003
alfred.com

Printed in USA.

ISBN-10: 1-4706-1071-X

ISBN-13: 978-1-4706-1071-5

Piano keys: © Shutterstock / Ensuper • Brush stroke: © Shutterstock / foxie • Celtic cross: © Shutterstock / vectorbomb

Contents

by Title

10,000 Reasons

(Bless the Lord)

Words and Music by
Matt Redman and Jonas Myrin
Arr. Carol Tornquist

Verse:

C/G   G   C   G   D   Em

1. The sun comes up, it's a new day dawn - ing.
2. You're rich in love and You're slow to an - ger. Your
3. *See additional lyrics.*

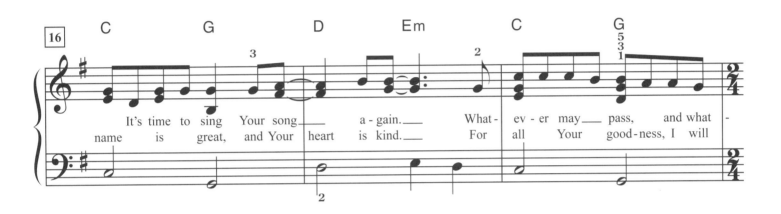

C   G   D   Em   C   G

It's time to sing Your song ___ a - gain. ___ What - ev - er may ___ pass, and what -
name is great, and Your heart is kind. ___ For all Your good - ness, I will

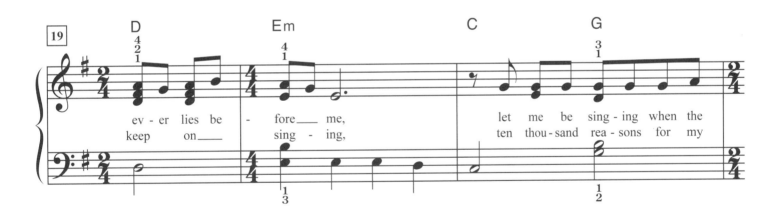

D   Em   C   G

ev - er lies be - fore ___ me, let me be sing - ing when the
keep on ___ sing - ing, ten thou - sand rea - sons for my

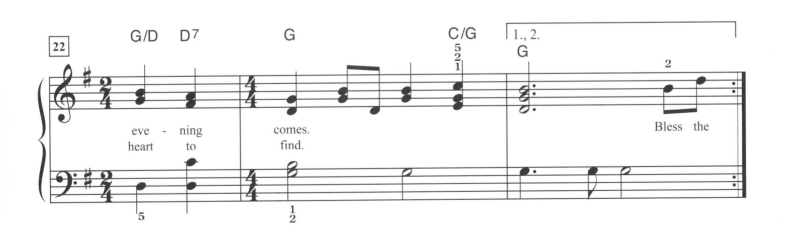

G/D   D7   G   C/G   1., 2. G

eve - ning comes. Bless the
heart to find.

Verse 3:
And on that day when my strength is failing,
The end draws near and my time has come;
Still, my soul will sing Your praise unending,
Ten thousand years and then forevermore.

Amazing Grace
(My Chains Are Gone)

Words and Music by
Chris Tomlin and Louie Giglio
Arr. Carol Tornquist

Moderately slow

with pedal

Verse:

1. A - maz - ing__ grace! how sweet the sound that

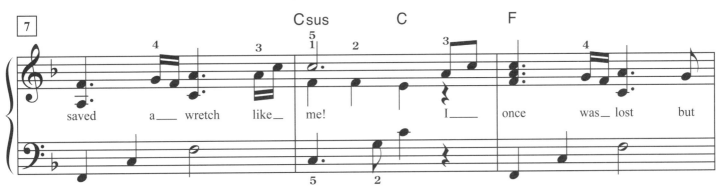

saved a__ wretch like__ me! I__ once was__ lost but

now am found; was blind, but__ now__ I see. My chains are

Above All

Words and Music by
Paul Baloche and Lenny Leblanc
Arr. Carol Tornquist

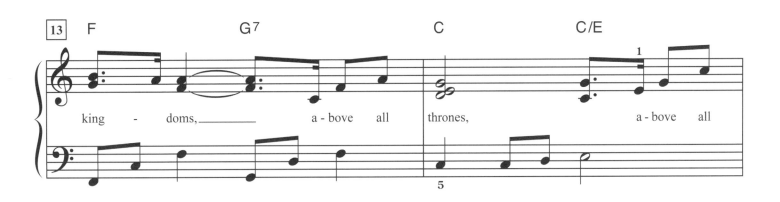

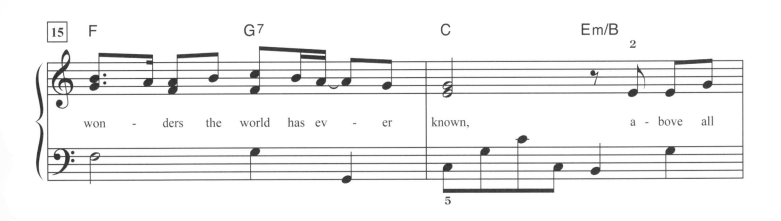

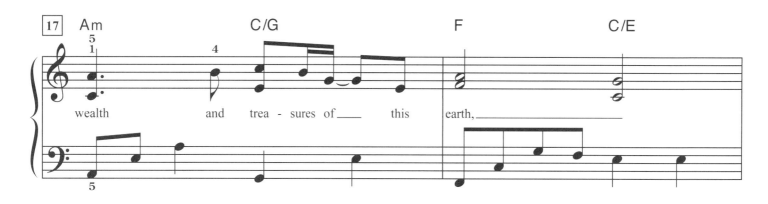

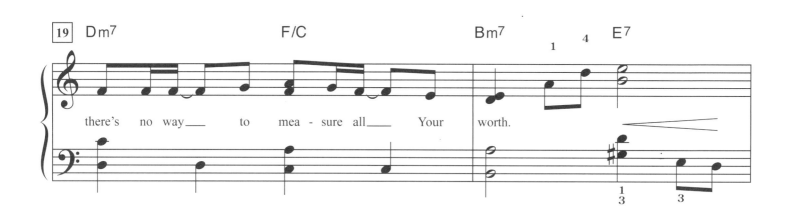

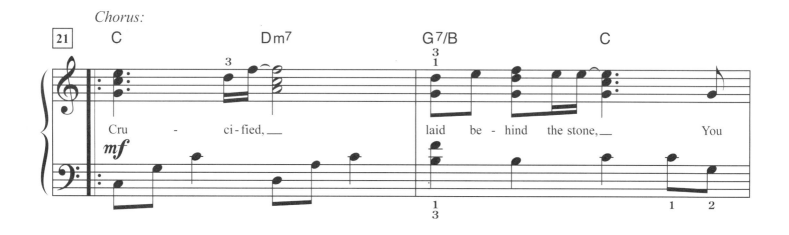

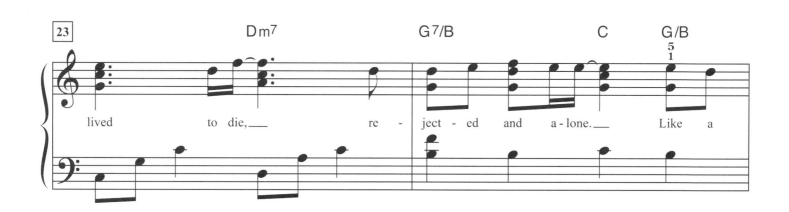

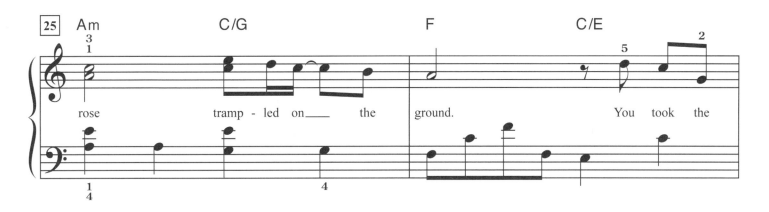

rose   tramp - led on___ the   ground.   You took the

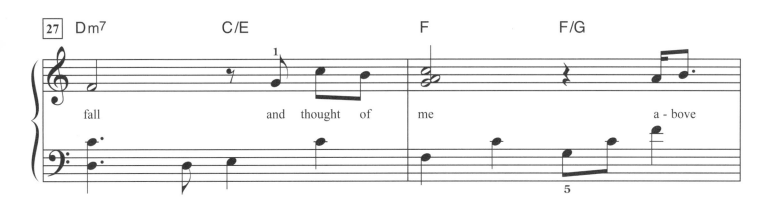

fall   and thought of   me   a - bove

all.

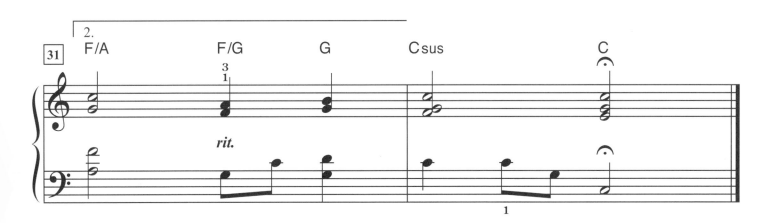

Blessed

Words and Music by Billie Hughes
Arr. Carol Tornquist

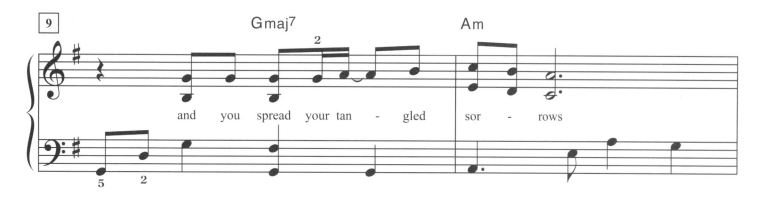

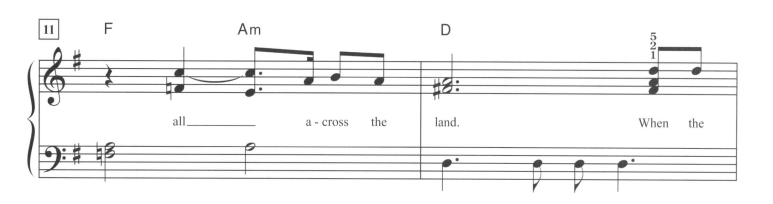

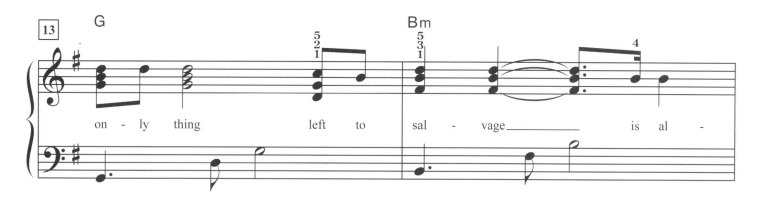

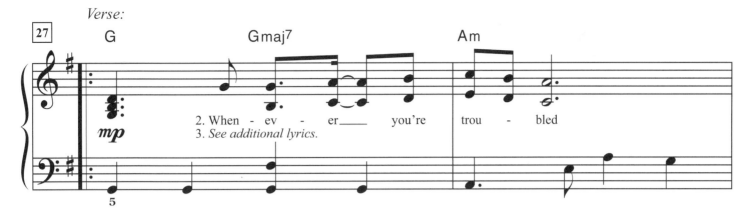

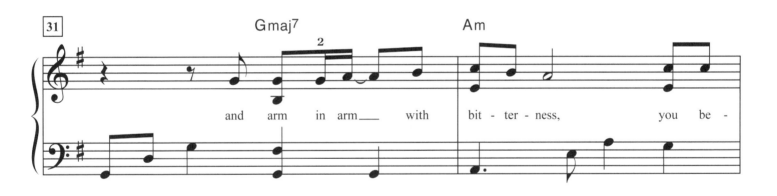

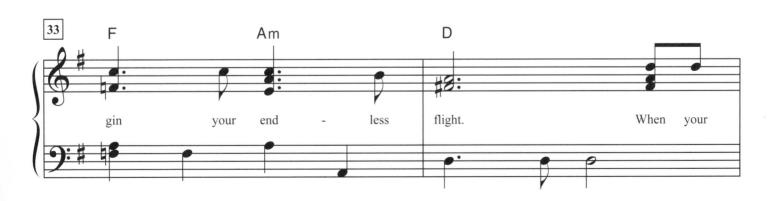

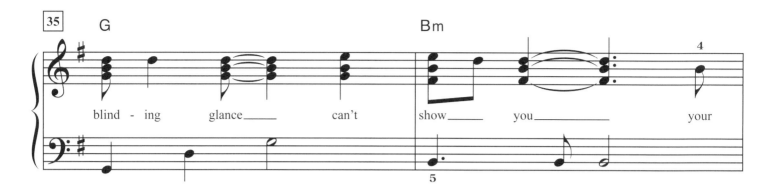

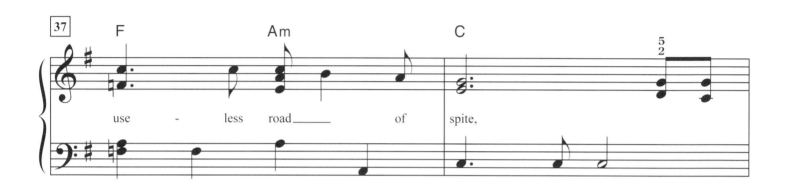

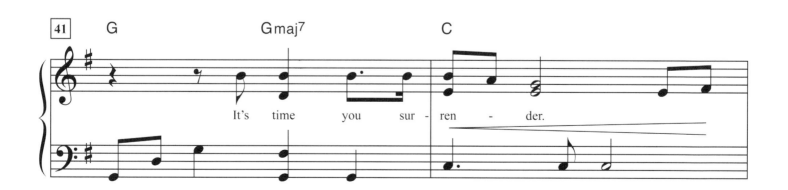

Verse 3:
When the Prophet's tongue lies silent in His mouth,
And your barren fields lie worthless all through the summer's drought,
And just when you feel for certain you can never find your way out,
Then it's time you remember.
It's time you surrender.
Blessed are those who wait upon the Lord.

Blessings

Words and Music by Laura Mixon Story
Arr. Carol Tornquist

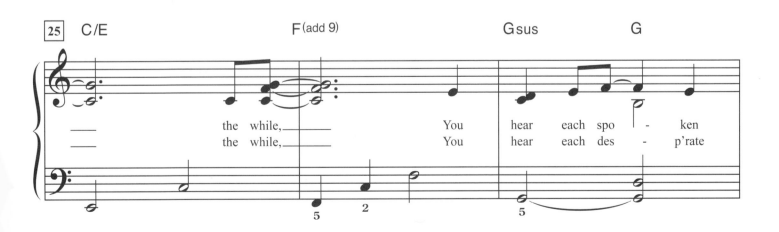

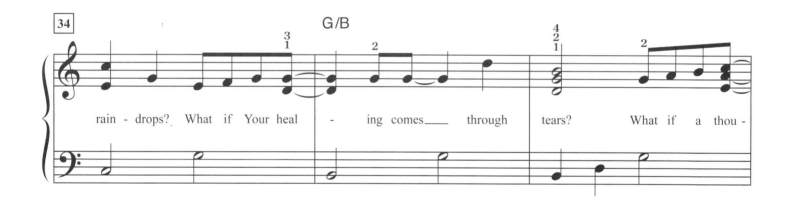

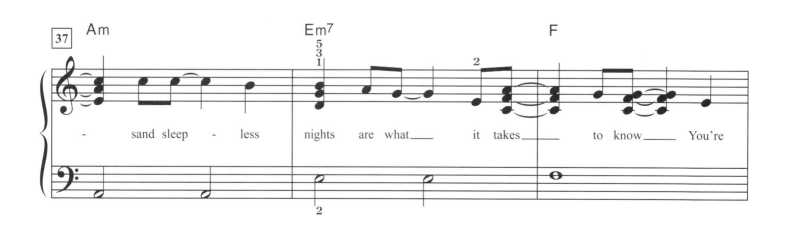

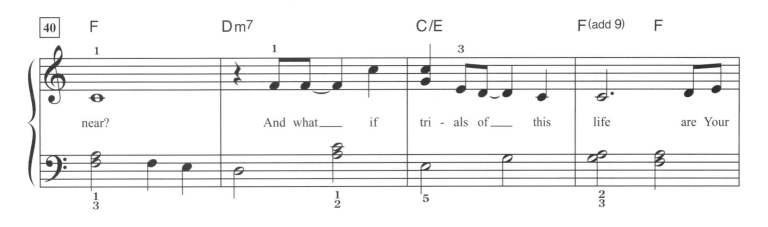

near? And what___ if tri - als of ___ this life are Your

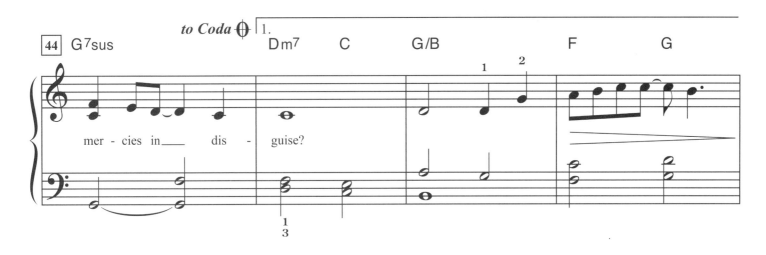

mer - cies in___ dis - guise?

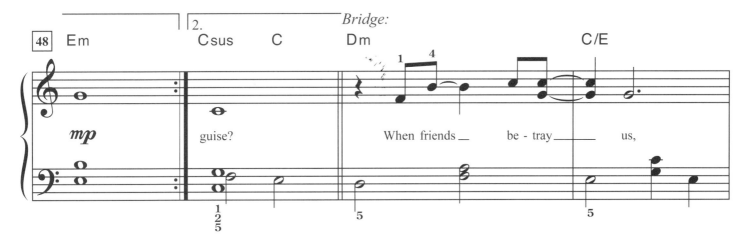

guise? When friends ___ be - tray___ us,

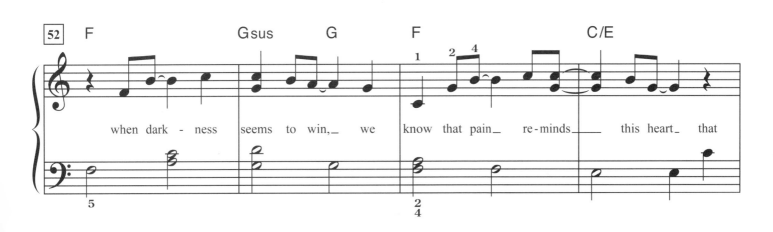

when dark - ness seems to win,___ we know that pain___ re - minds___ this heart___ that

Cinderella

Words and Music by
Steven Curtis Chapman
Arr. Carol Tornquist

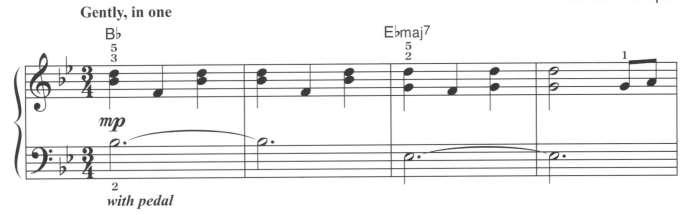

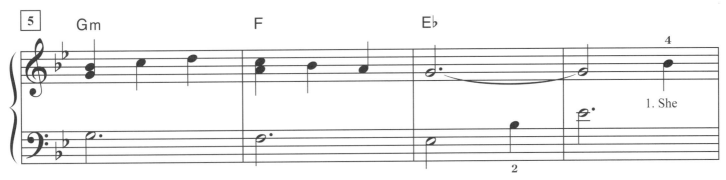

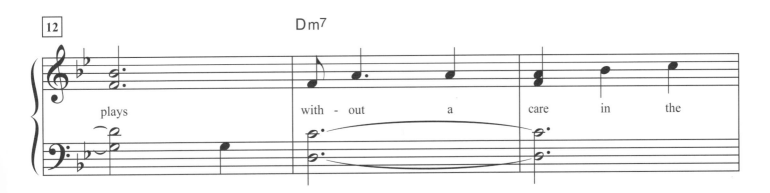

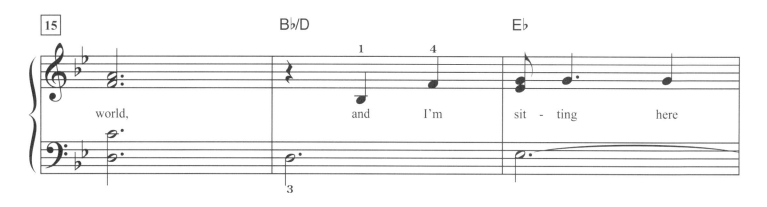

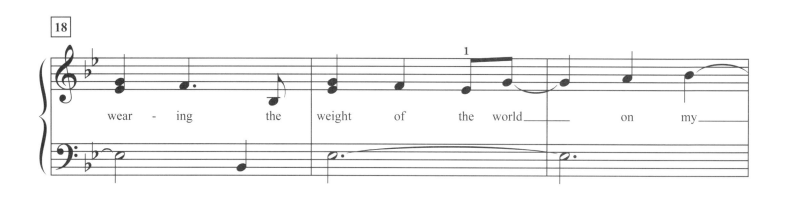

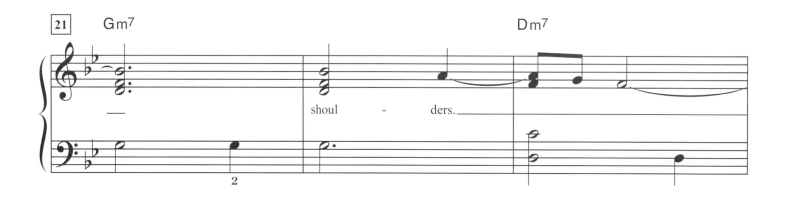

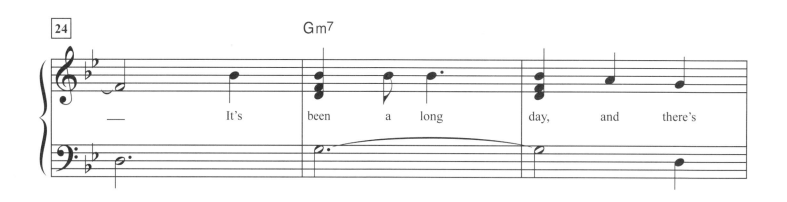

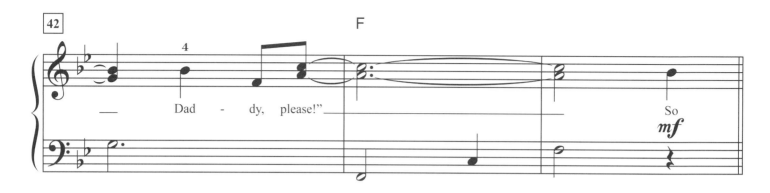

Chorus:

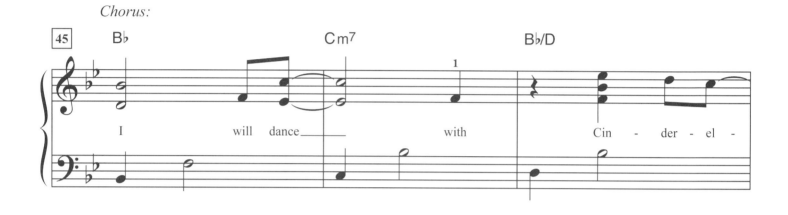

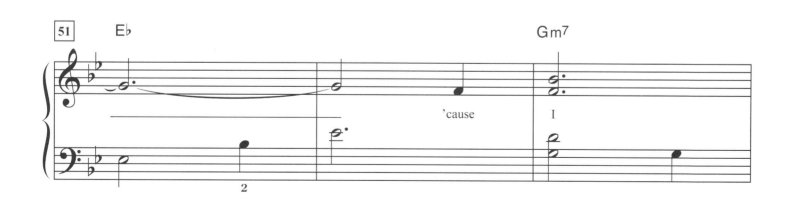

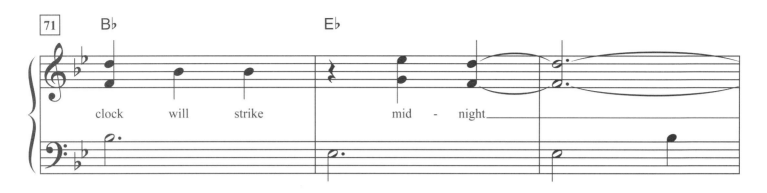

clock will strike mid - night

and she'll

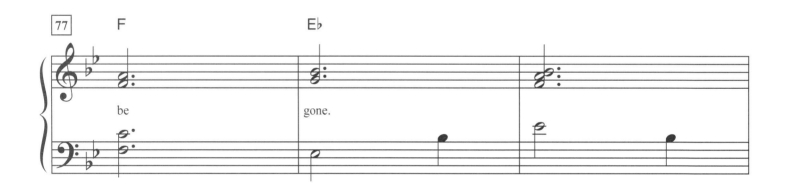

be gone.

mp
1., 2.
3.
1. She
3. Well,

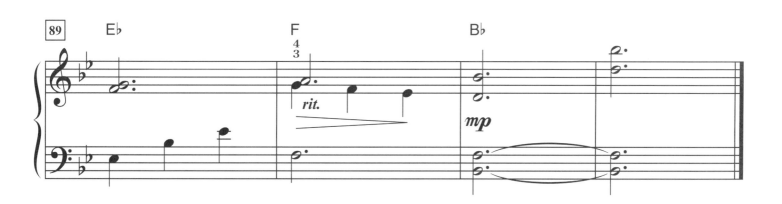

Verse 2:
She says he's a nice guy and I'd be impressed;
She wants to know if I approve of her dress.
She says, "Dad, the prom is just one week away,
And I need to practice my dancing.
Oh, please, Daddy, please!"
(To Chorus:)

Verse 3:
Well, she came home today with a ring on her hand,
Just glowing, and telling all they had planned.
She says, "Dad, the wedding's still six months away,
but I need to practice my dancing.
Oh, please, Daddy, please!"
(To Chorus:)

God's Not Dead
(Like a Lion)

Words and Music by Daniel Bashta
Arr. Carol Tornquist

Chorus:

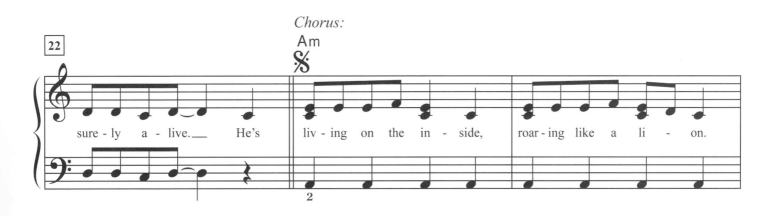

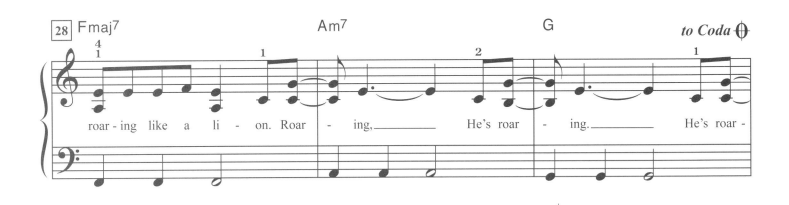

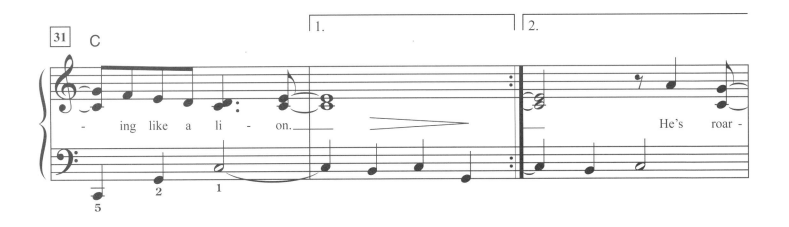

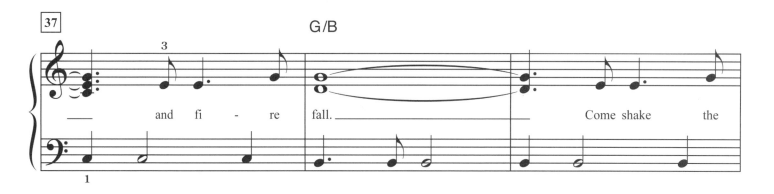

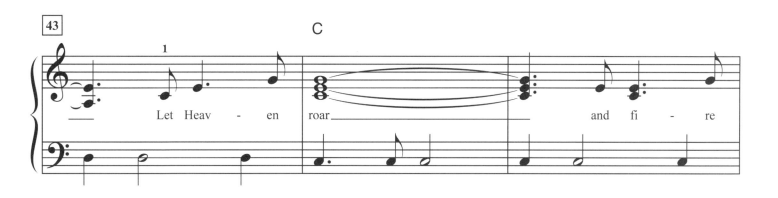

Good Morning

Words and Music by Aaron Rice, Cary Barlowe,
Jamie Moore, Mandisa Hundley and Toby McKeehan
Arr. Carol Tornquist

Bridge:

29 Gm7 ... Dm7 ... Am7

Now I'm smil-ing and I'm kiss-ing all my wor-ries good-bye.___ Got the feel-ing if I

32 Em7 ... Gm7 ... Dm7

spread my wings, I might e-ven fly.___ You are my truth, my way.___ Give me the strength to say,

35 B♭

"Get up, get up, get up!"___ Oh, 'cause it's a good morn - ing.

38 C7sus — *D.S. al Coda*

'Cause it's a good

Coda

B♭ ... Csus ... F

rit.

Verse 2:
Slow down, breathe in, don't move ahead.
I'm just living in the moment.
I've got my arms raised, unphased, jump out of bed.
Gotta get this party going.
I went to bed dreaming.
You woke me up singing, "Get up, get up, hey!"
(To Chorus:)

Hold Me

Words and Music by Chris Stevens,
Jamie Grace and Toby McKeehan
Arr. Carol Tornquist

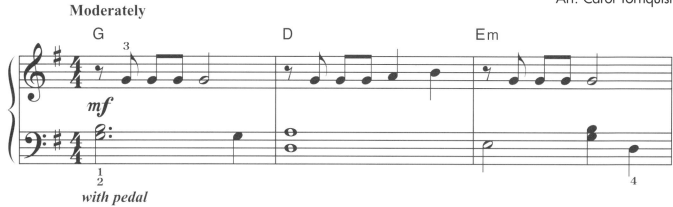

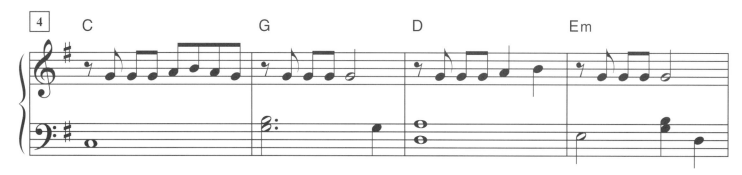

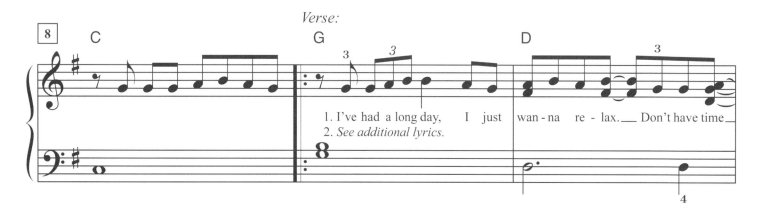

1. I've had a long day, I just wan-na re-lax. Don't have time
2. See additional lyrics.

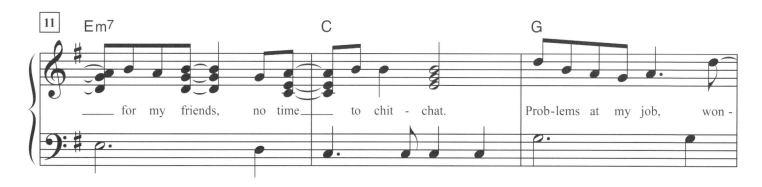

___ for my friends, no time___ to chit - chat. Prob-lems at my job, won-

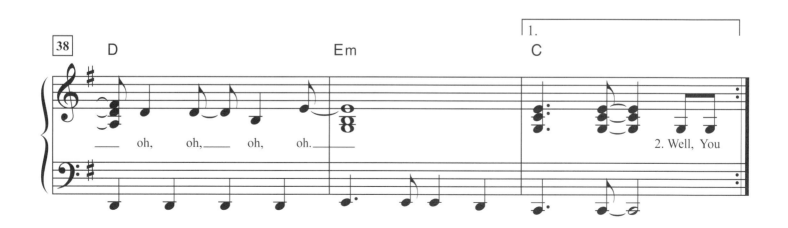

Verse 2:
Well, You took my day and You flipped it around,
Calmed the tidal wave and put my feet on the ground.
Forever in my heart, always on my mind,
It's crazy how I think about you all of the time.
And just when I think I'm 'bout to figure You out,
You make me wanna sing and shout.
(To Chorus:)

How Beautiful

Words and Music by Twila Paris
Arr. Carol Tornquist

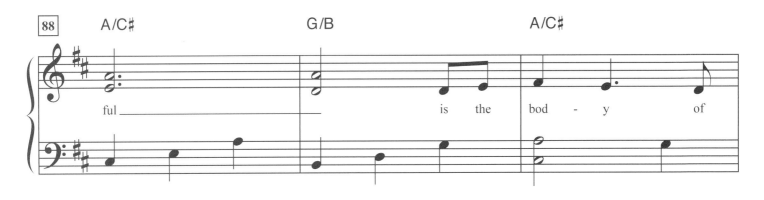

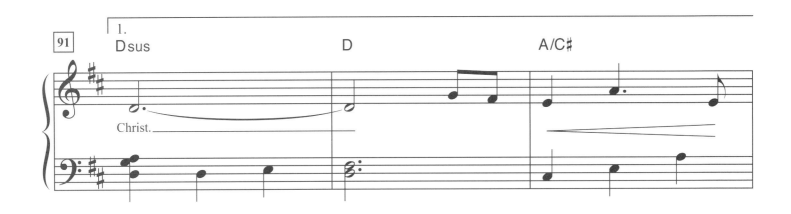

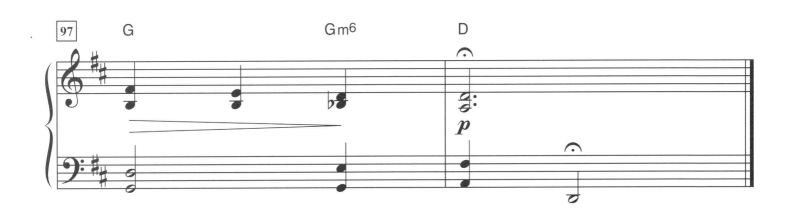

I Need a Miracle

Words and Music by David Carr,
Mac Powell, Mark Lee and Tai Anderson
Arr. Carol Tornquist

Verse 2:
He lost his job and all he had in the fall of '09.
Now he feared the worst, that he would lose his children and his wife.
So he drove down deep into the woods and thought he'd end it all,
And prayed, "Lord above, I need a miracle."
(To Chorus:)

Verse 3:
He turned on the radio to hear a song for the last time.
He didn't know what he was looking for or even what he'd find.
And the song he heard, it gave him hope and strength to carry on.
And on that night they found a miracle.
(To Chorus:)

How Great Is Our God

Words and Music by Jesse Reeves,
Chris Tomlin and Ed Cash
Arr. Carol Tornquist

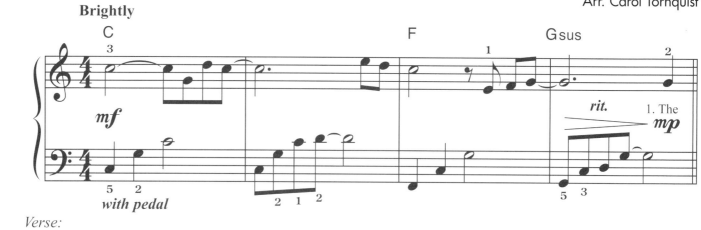

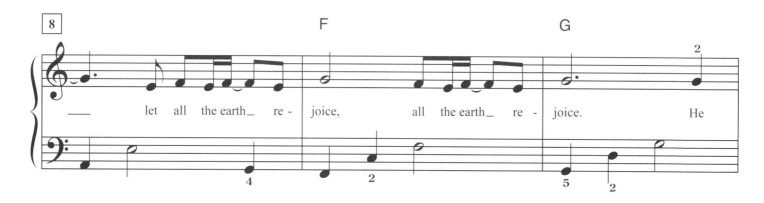

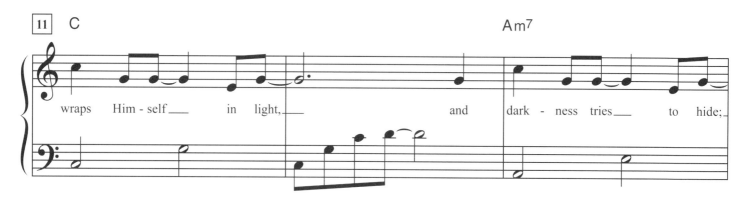

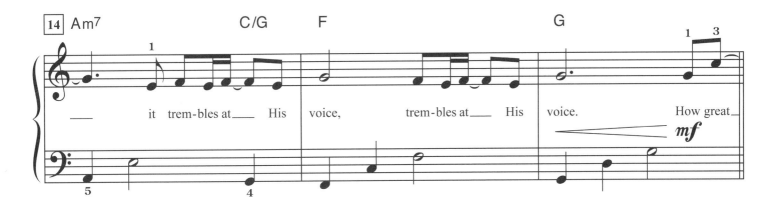

Chorus:

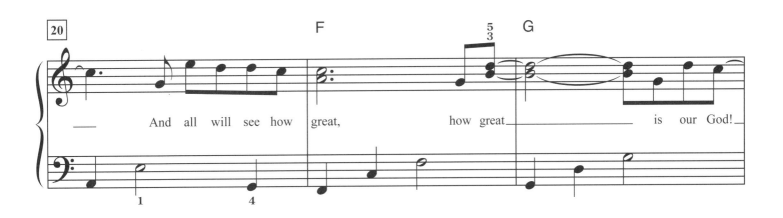

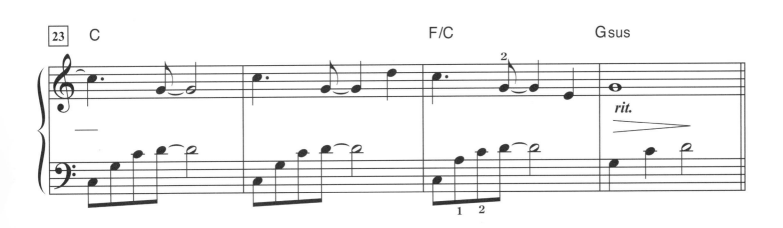

Verse:
a tempo

2. Age to age___ He stands,___ and time is in___ His hands;

___ Be - gin - ning and___ the End, Be - gin - ning and___ the End. The

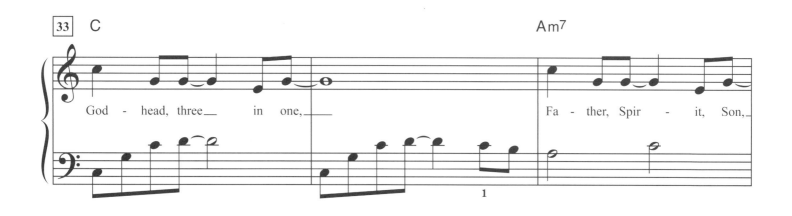

God - head, three___ in one,___ Fa - ther, Spir - it, Son,

___ the Li - on and___ the Lamb, the Li - on and___ the Lamb. How great___

Chorus:

is our God! Sing with me, "How great is our God!"

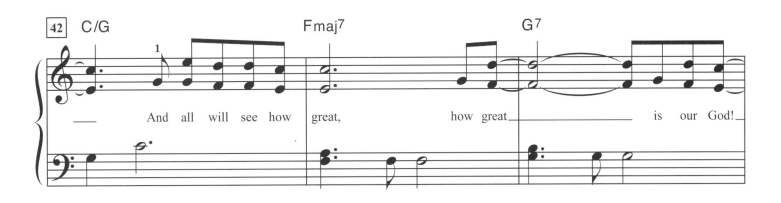

And all will see how great, how great is our God!

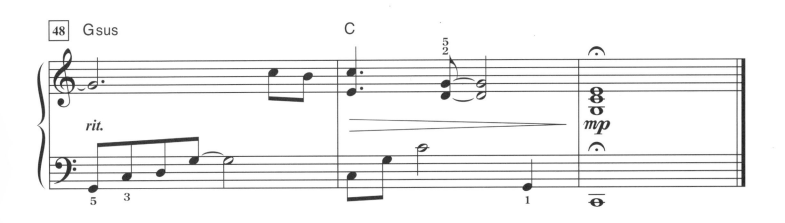

How He Loves

Words and Music by John Mark McMillan
Arr. Carol Tornquist

all of a sud - den   I am un - a - ware of these af - flic - tions e - clipsed by

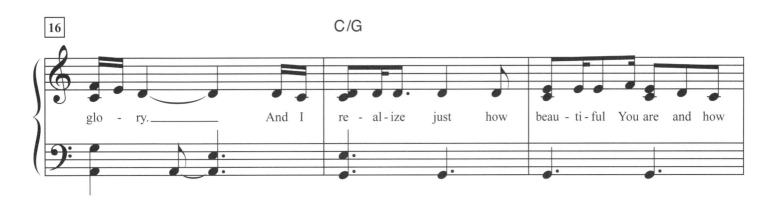

glo - ry._____   And I   re - al - ize   just   how   beau - ti - ful You are   and how

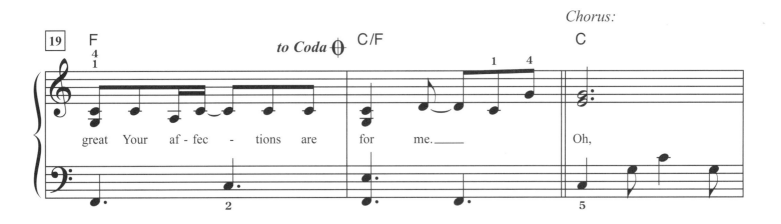

great Your af - fec - tions are   for   me._____   Oh,

how He__ loves us.___ Oh,   oh,   how He___

loves___ us,___ how He___ loves us___ all.

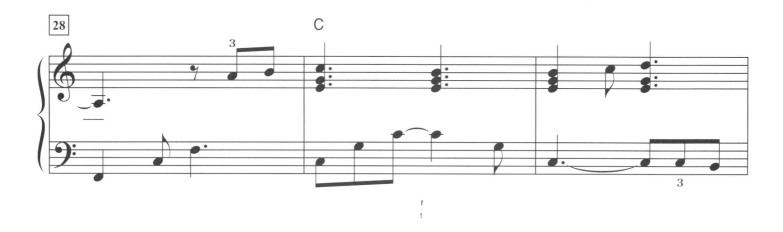

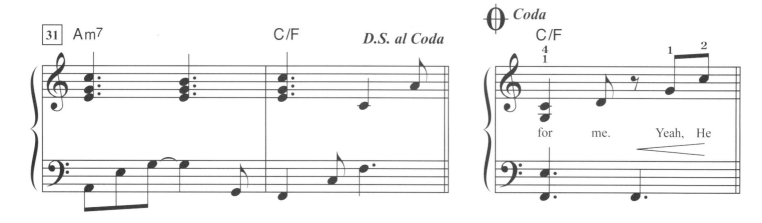

D.S. al Coda

Coda

for me. Yeah, He

Chorus:

loves us. Oh,_____ how He loves us.

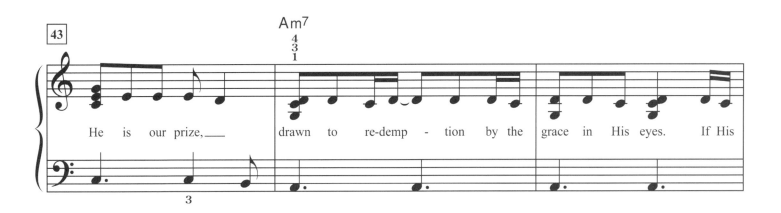

And heav-en meets earth like an un-fore-seen kiss and my

heart turns vio-lent-ly in - side of my chest. I don't have time to main-

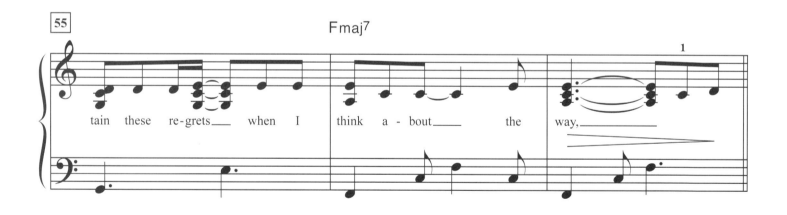

tain these re-grets___ when I think a-bout___ the way,___

Chorus:

Oh, how He___ loves us.___ Oh,

I Can Only Imagine

Words and Music by Bart Millard
Arr. Carol Tornquist

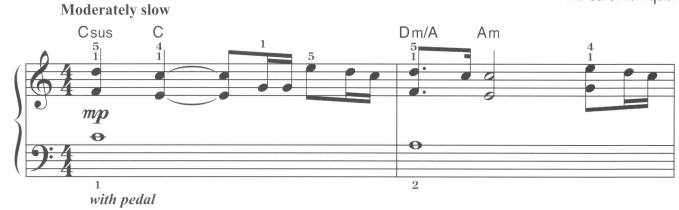

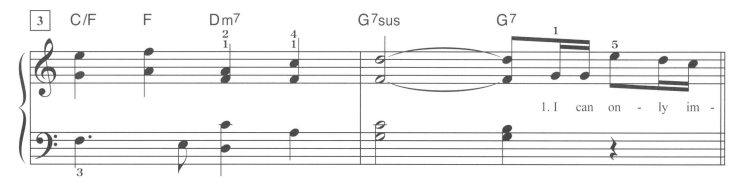

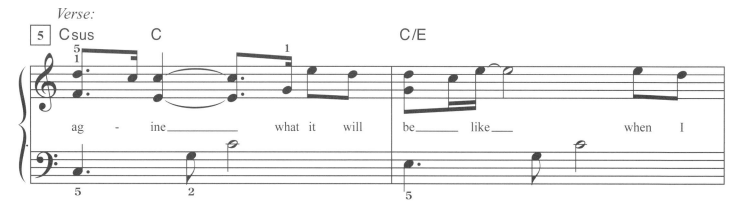

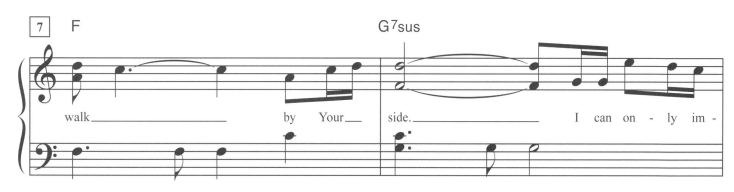

I Will Rise

Words and Music by Chris Tomlin,
Jesse Reeves, Louie Giglio and Matt Maher
Arr. Carol Tornquist

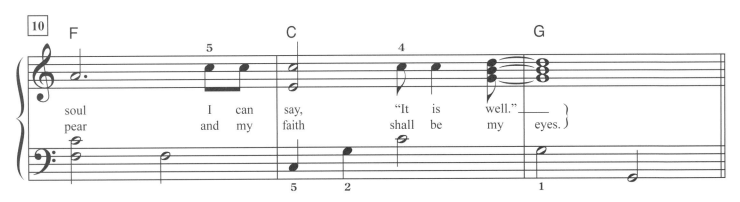

In Christ Alone

Words and Music by
Stuart Townend and Keith Getty
Arr. Carol Tornquist

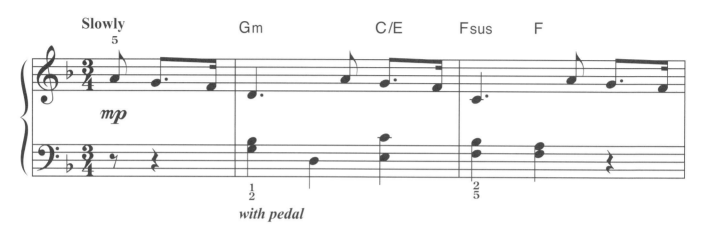

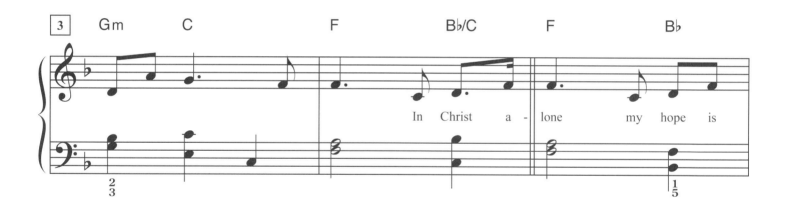

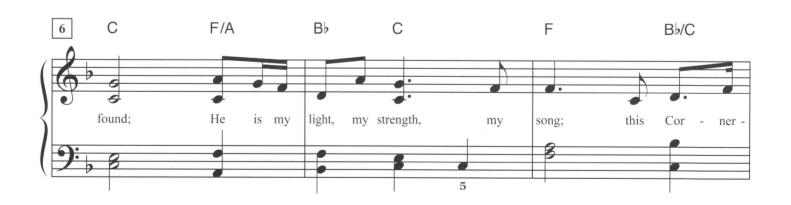

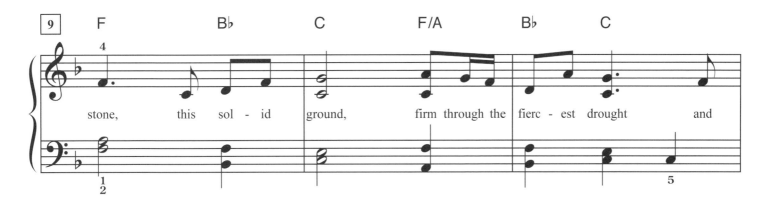

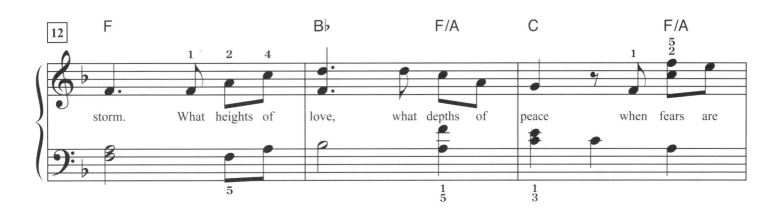

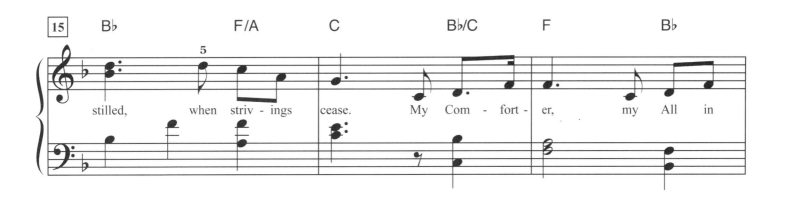

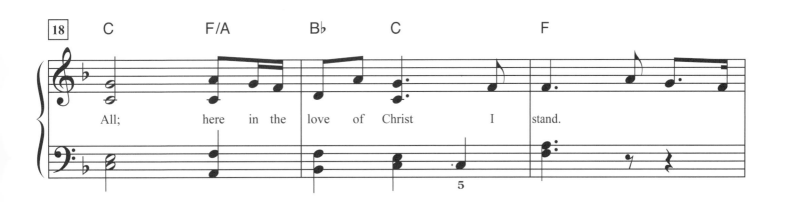

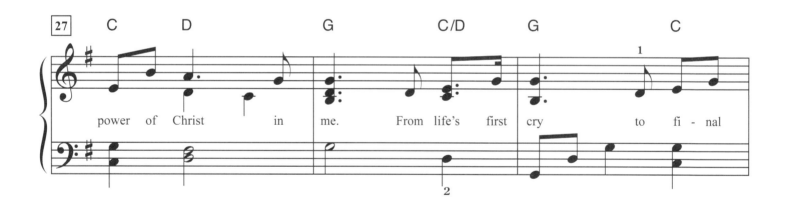

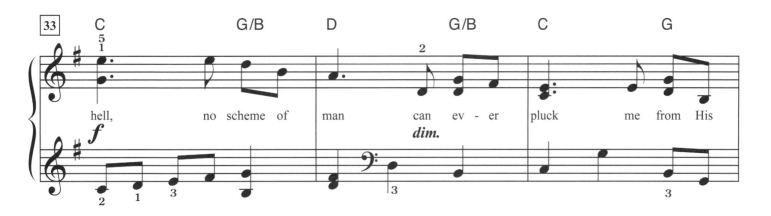

hell, no scheme of man can ev-er pluck me from His

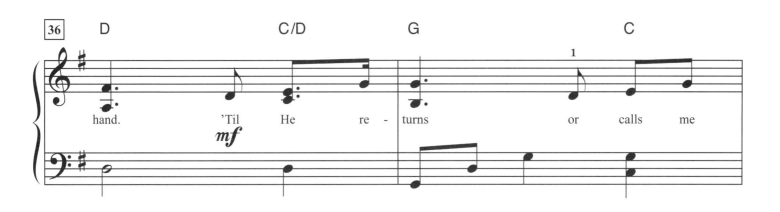

hand. 'Til He re-turns or calls me

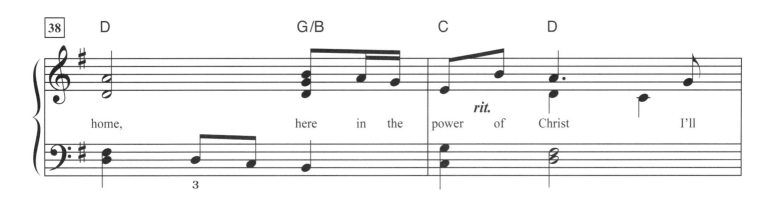

home, here in the power of Christ I'll

Very slowly

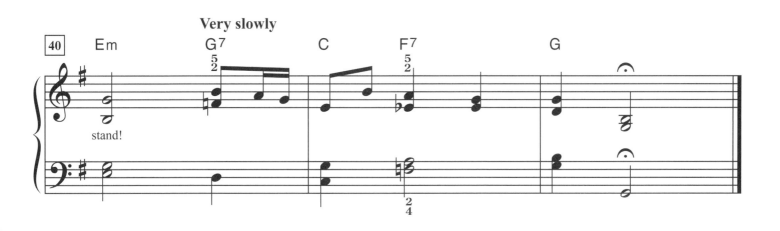

stand!

Jesus, Friend of Sinners

Words and Music by
Matthew West and Mark Hall
Arr. Carol Tornquist

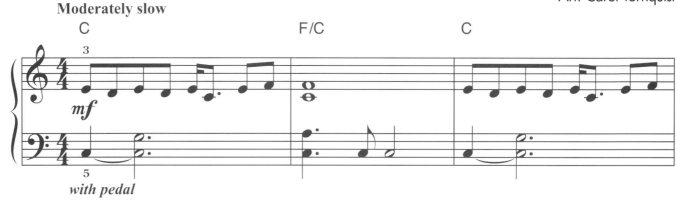

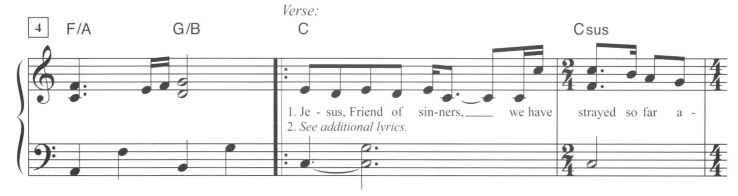

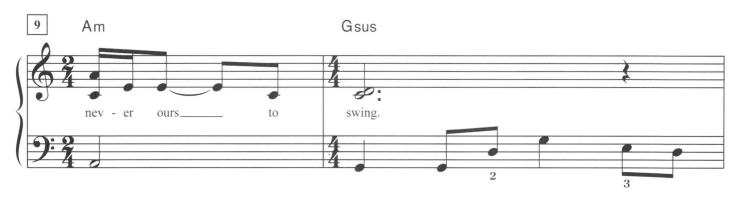

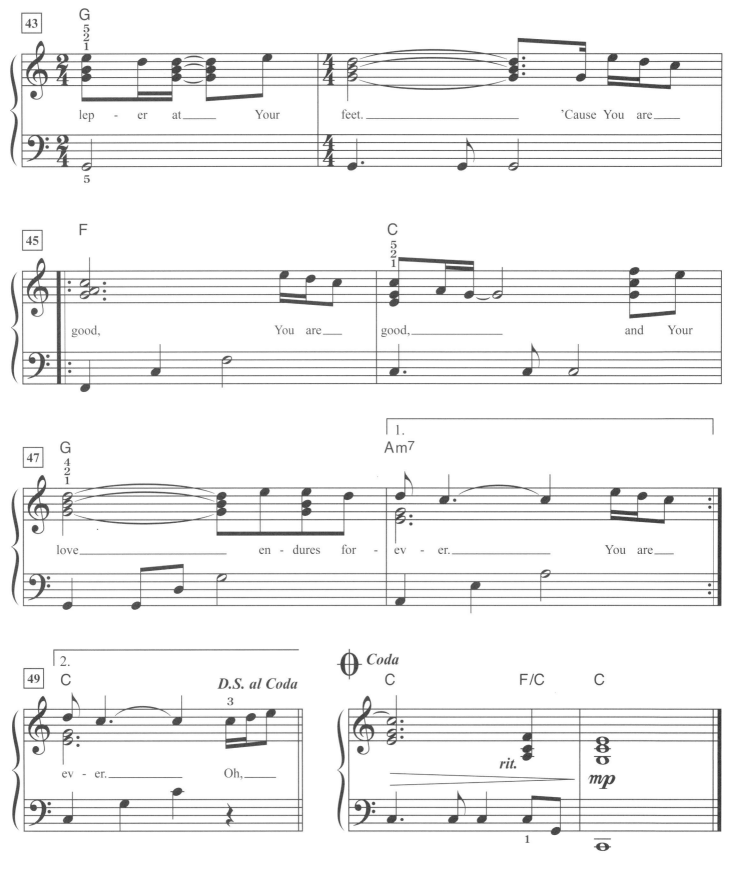

Verse 2:
Jesus, Friend of sinners, the One whose writing in the sand
Made the righteous turn away and the stones fall from their hands,
Help us to remember we are all the least of these.
Let the memory of Your mercy bring Your people to their knees.
Nobody knows what we're for, only what we're against when we judge the wounded.
What if we put down our signs, crossed over the lines and loved like You did?
(To Chorus:)

Need You Now

(How Many Times)

Words and Music by Christa Wells,
Luke Sheets and Tiffany Arbuckle
Arr. Carol Tornquist

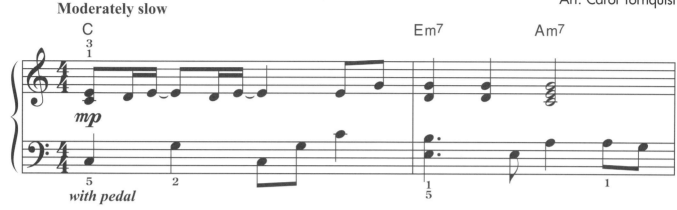

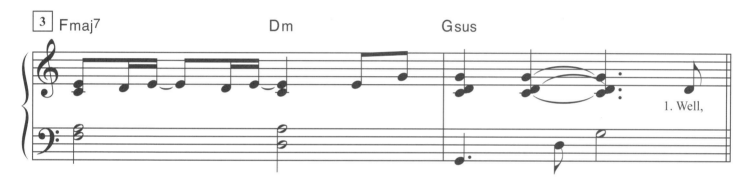

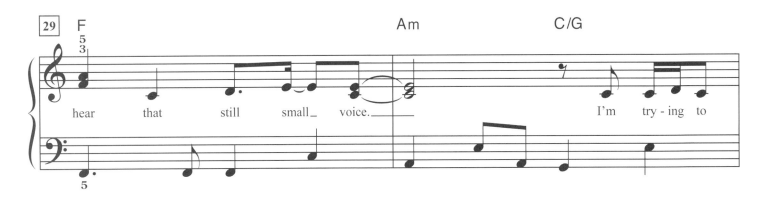

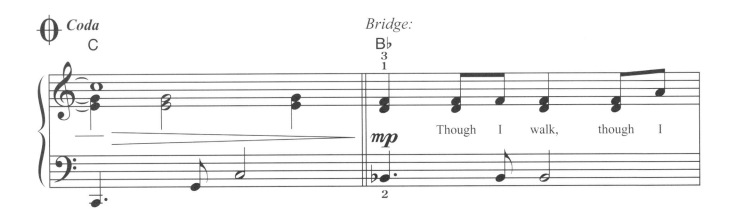

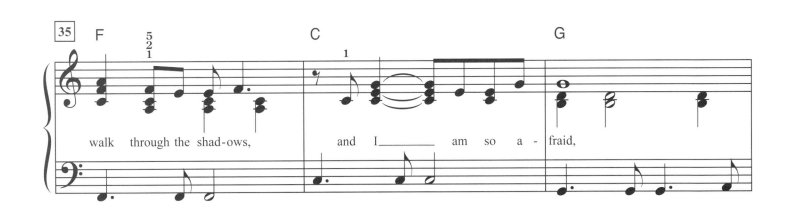

Let the Church Say Amen

Words and Music by Andrae Crouch
Arr. Carol Tornquist

Moderately slow, with a steady beat

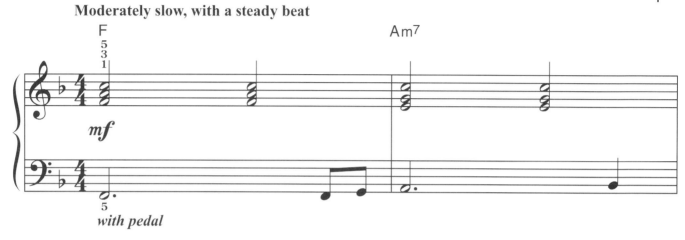

with pedal

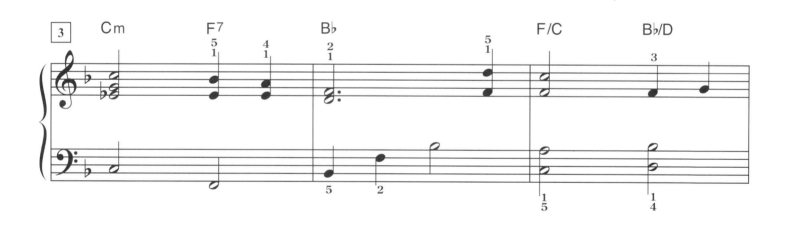

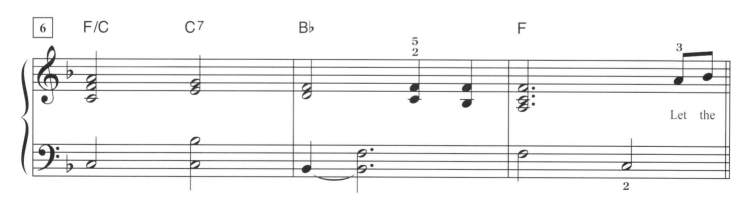

Let the

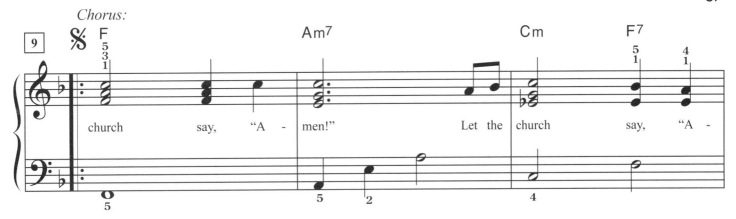

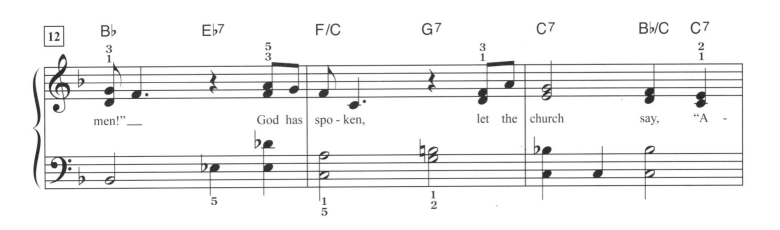

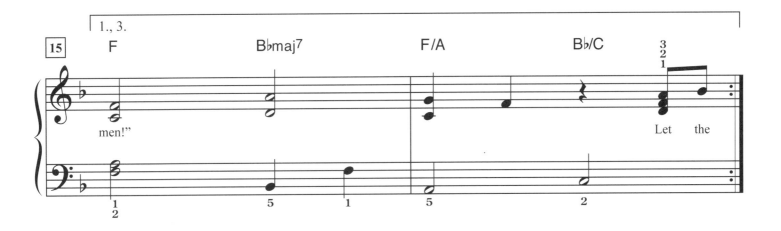

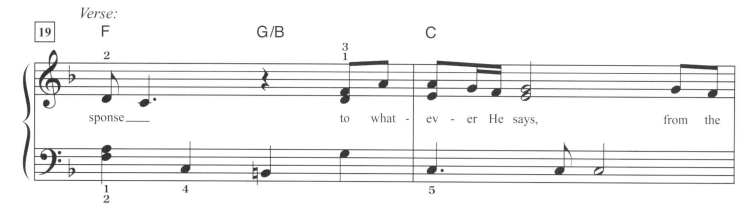

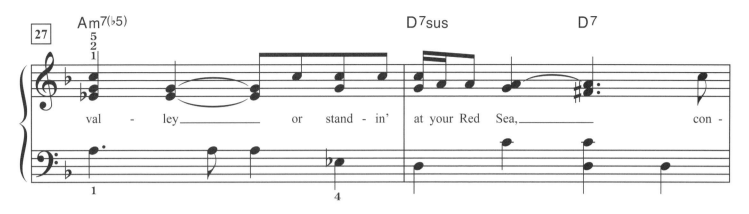

val - ley_____ or stand - in' at your Red Sea,_____ con -

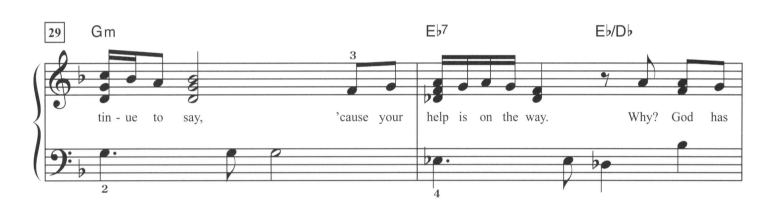

tin - ue to say, 'cause your help is on the way. Why? God has

spo - ken, I heard Him. So let the church say,_____ "A -

men!" Let the men!" He can

Chorus:

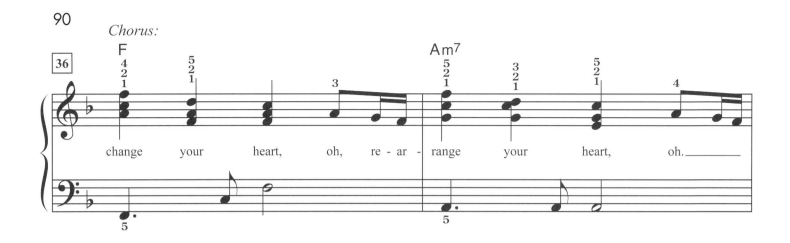

change your heart, oh, re-ar-range your heart, oh._____

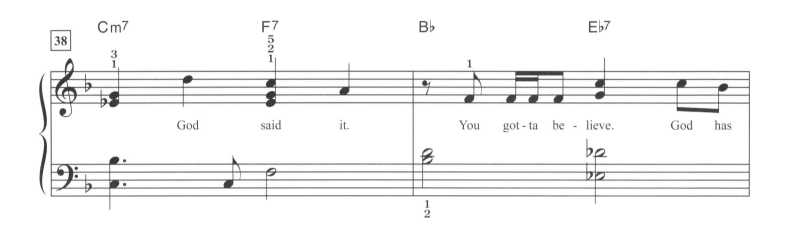

God said it. You got-ta be-lieve. God has

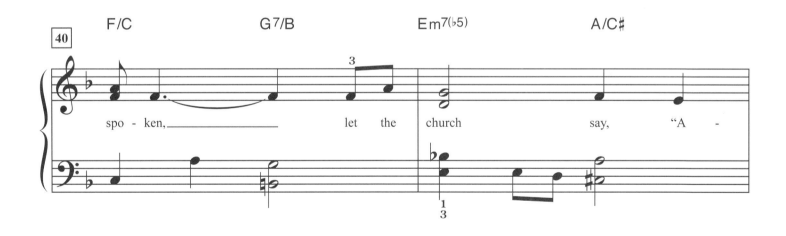

spo-ken,_____ let the church say, "A-

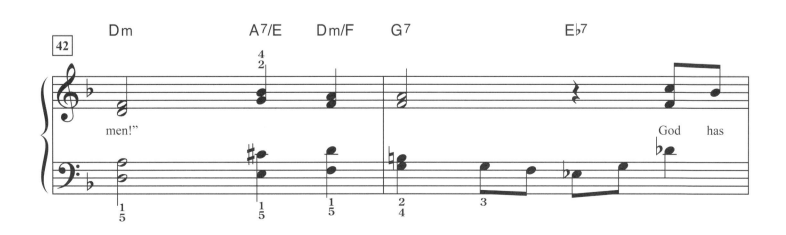

men!" God has

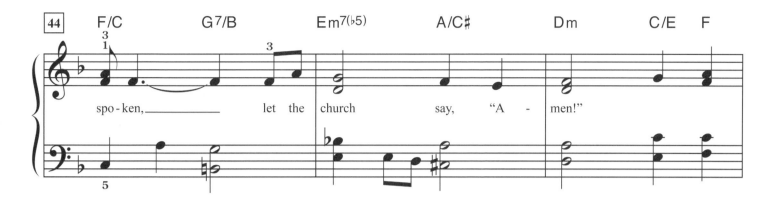

spo - ken,_____ let the church say, "A - men!"

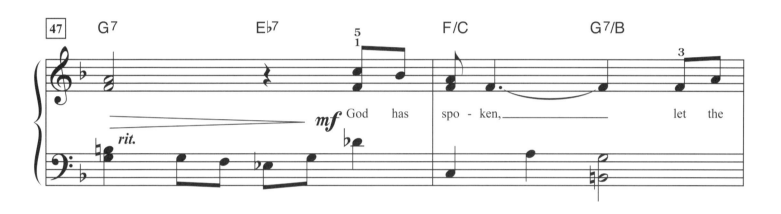

mf God has spo - ken,_____ let the

rit.

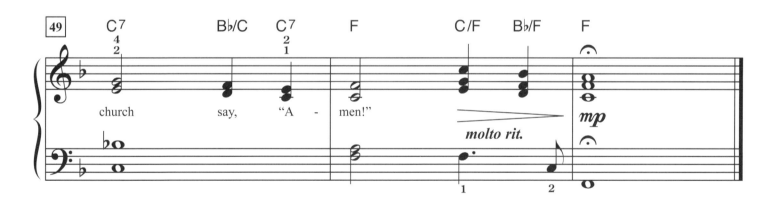

church say, "A - men!"

molto rit.

Verse 2:

When your dream's about to die, knowing that God is not a man, He just can't lie.
In spite of what, what the devil does, no, you got a word that has come from above.
Faith must be, must be what you say, so open your mouth and say, "Amen" today.
'Cause God, I heard Him when He said it. So let the church say, "Amen!"
(To Chorus):

One Thing Remains
(Your Love Never Fails)

Words and Music by Jeremy Riddle,
Brian Johnson and Christa Black
Arr. Carol Tornquist

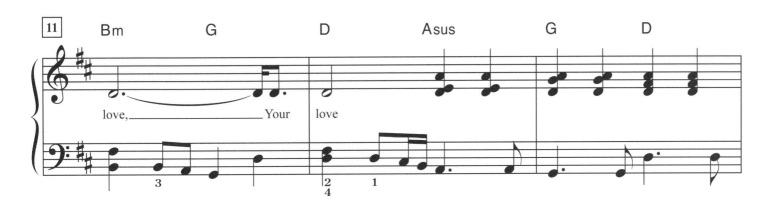

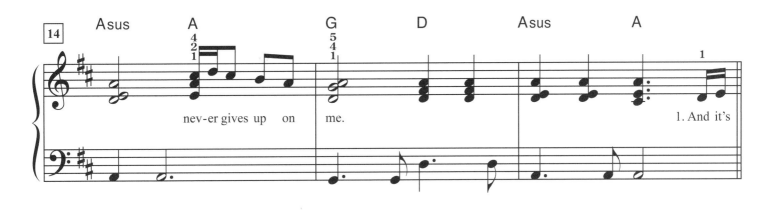

Verse:

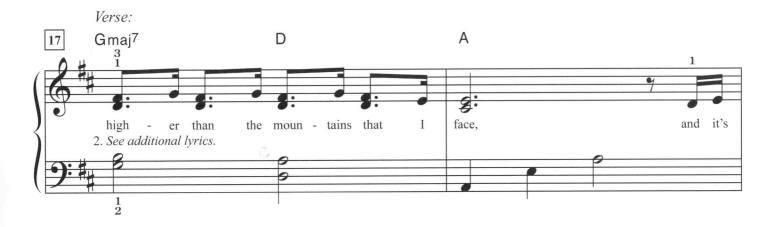

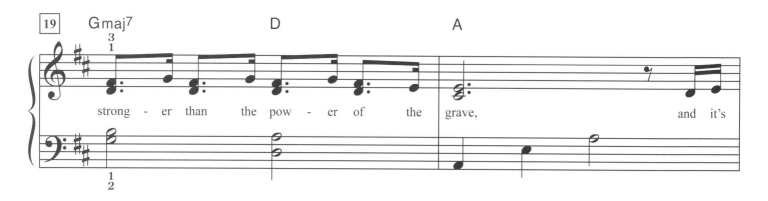

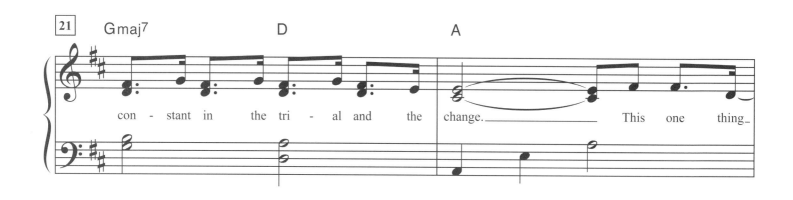

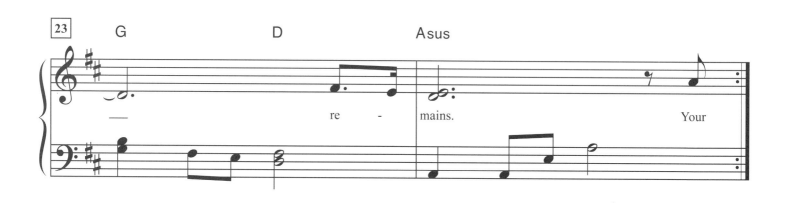

Chorus:

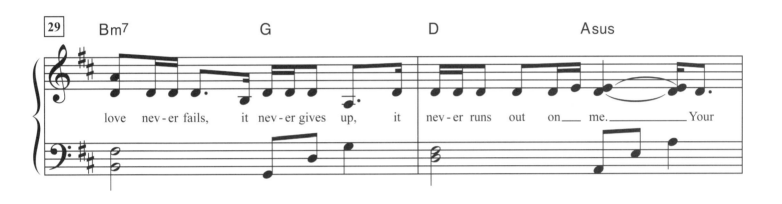

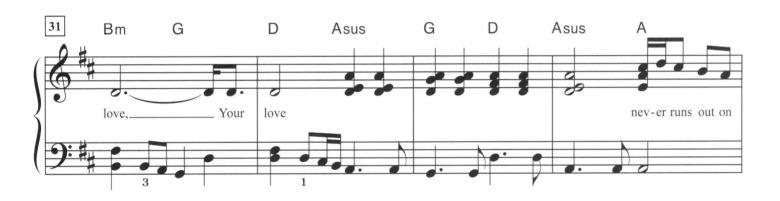

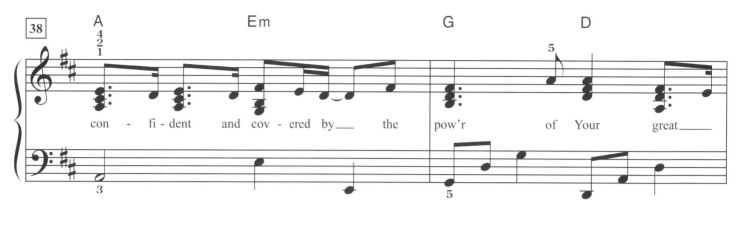

Verse 2:
And on and on and on and on it goes.
Yes, it overwhelms and satisfies my soul.
And I'll never, ever have to be afraid.
This one thing remains.
(To Chorus:)

The Prayer

Words and Music by
Carole Bayer Sager and David Foster
Arr. Carol Tornquist

The Proof of Your Love

Words and Music by Luke Smallbone, Joel David Smallbone,
Ben Glover, Frederick Williams, Jonathan Lee, and Mia Fieldes
Arr. Carol Tornquist

Verse:

give   to   a   need-y   soul   but   don't   have   love,   then   who   is   poor?   It

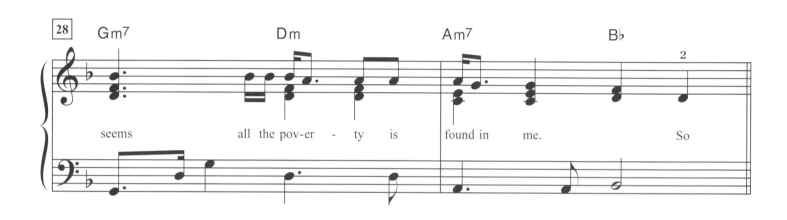

seems   all   the   pov-er   —   ty   is   found   in   me.   So

Chorus:

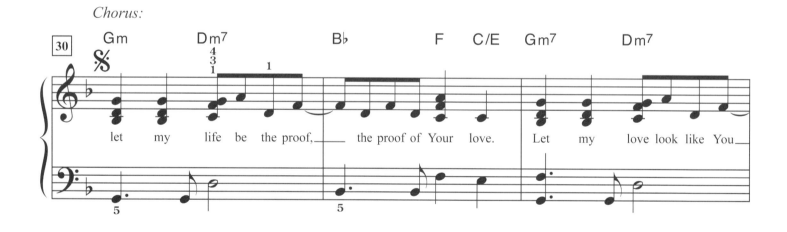

let   my   life   be   the   proof,   the   proof   of   Your   love.   Let   my   love   look   like   You

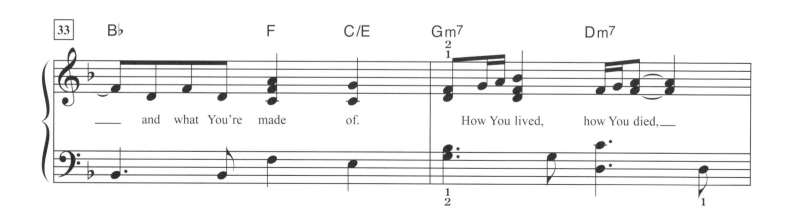

     and   what   You're   made   of.   How   You   lived,   how   You   died, __

love is sac - ri - fice. So let my life be the proof,___ the proof of Your love.

Bridge:

Whoa,_____ when it's all said and done, whoa,_____

when we sing our fi - nal song,_____ on - ly love re - mains, on - ly love re - mains._

Redeemed

Words and Music by
Benji Cowart and Michael Weaver
Arr. Carol Tornquist

Revelation Song

Words and Music by Jennie Lee Riddle
Arr. Carol Tornquist

come. With all cre-a-tion I sing praise to the King of kings.

You are my ev-'ry-thing, and I will a-dore You.

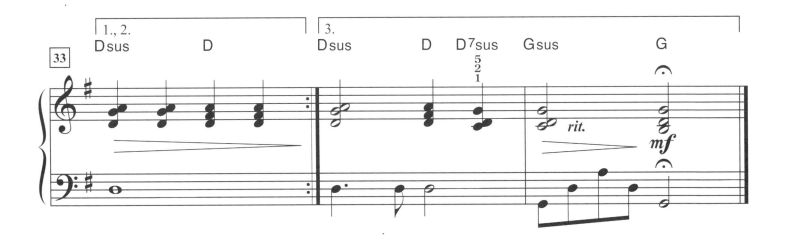

Verse 2:
Clothed in rainbows of living color,
Flashes of lightning, rolls of thunder,
Blessing and honor, strength and glory and power
Be to You, the only wise King.
(To Chorus:)

Verse 3:
Filled with wonder, awestruck wonder,
At the mention of Your name.
Jesus, Your name is power, breath, and living water,
Such a marvelous mystery.
(To Chorus:)

Shout to the Lord

Words and Music by Darlene Zschech
Arr. Carol Tornquist

name.___ I sing for joy___ at the work___ of Your hands.___ For -

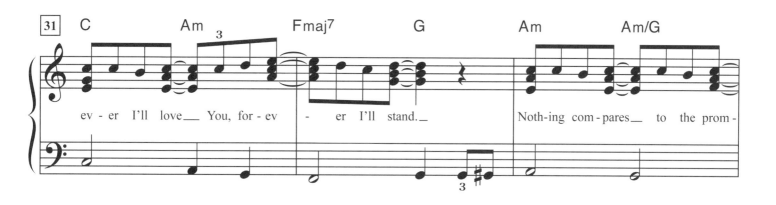

ev - er I'll love___ You, for - ev - er I'll stand.___ Noth-ing com-pares___ to the prom -

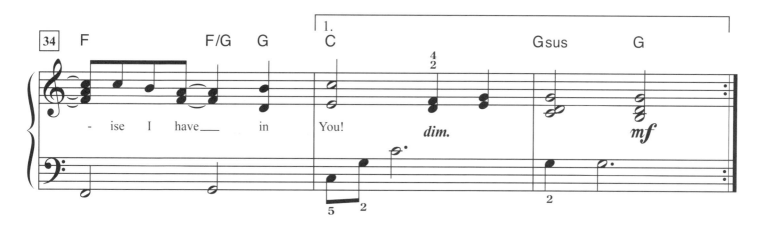

- ise I have___ in You! *dim.* *mf*

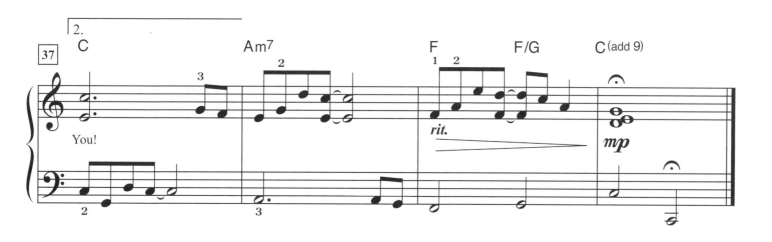

You! *rit.* *mp*

Take Me Back

Words and Music by Andrae Crouch
Arr. Carol Tornquist

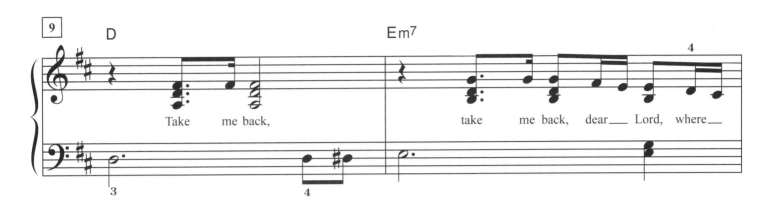

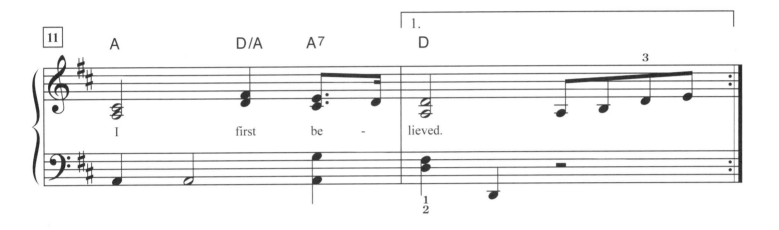

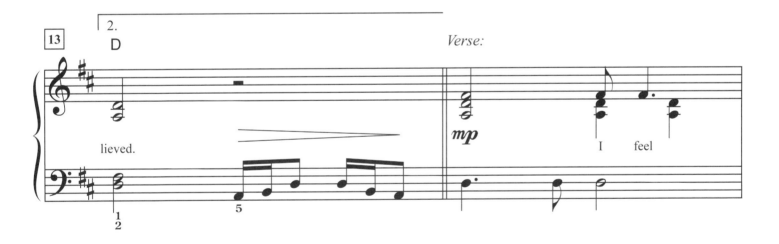

Take Me to the King

Words and Music by Kirk Franklin
Arr. Carol Tornquist

Verse:

tired,_____ op-tions are few._____ I'm tryin' to pray,_____ but__where are

You?_____ I'm all churched out,_____ hurt and a - bused._____ I

can't fake what's left to do. 2. Truth is, I'm__ weak,_____ no strength to

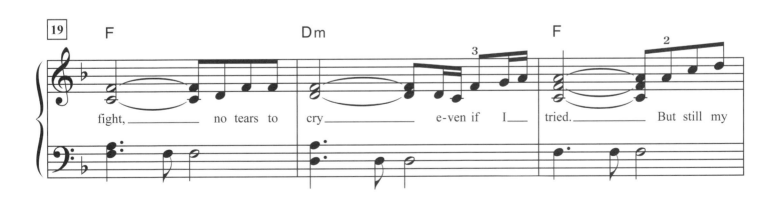

fight,_____ no tears to cry_____ e-ven if I___ tried._____ But still my

Chorus:

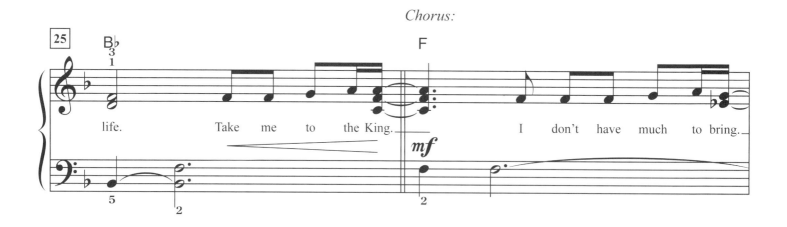

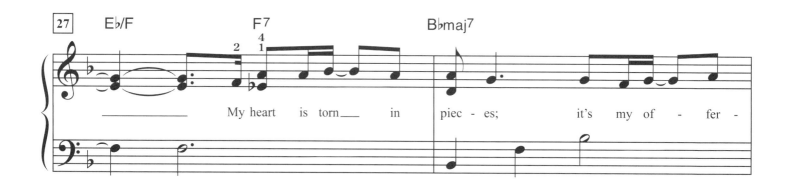

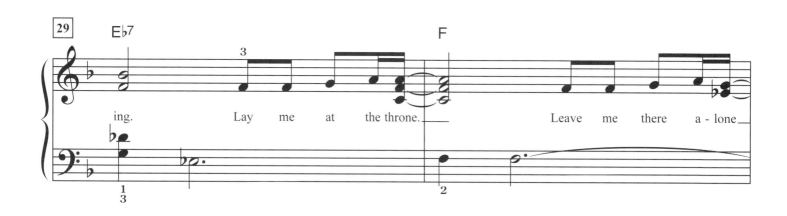

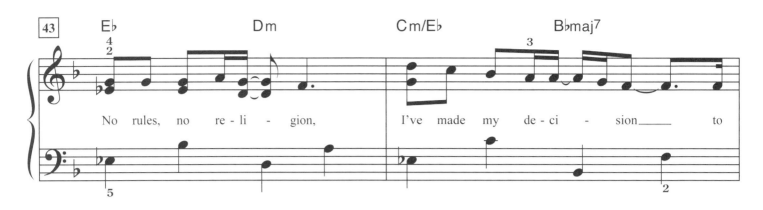

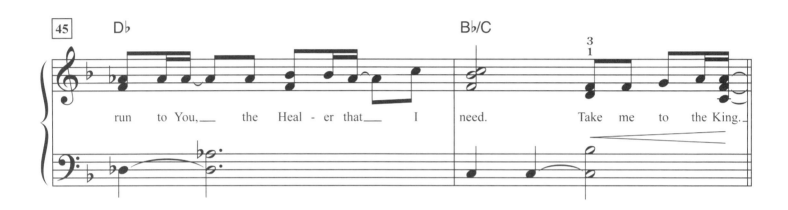

Chorus:

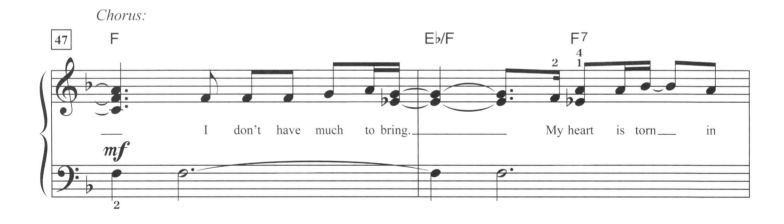

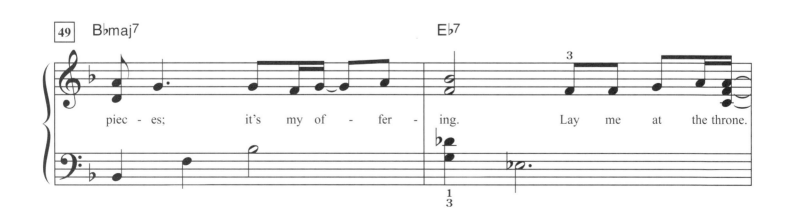

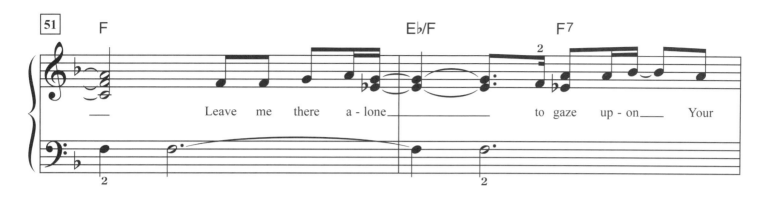

Leave me there a-lone_____ to gaze up-on___ Your

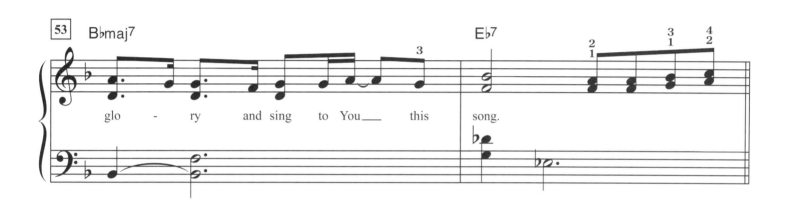

glo - ry and sing to You___ this song.

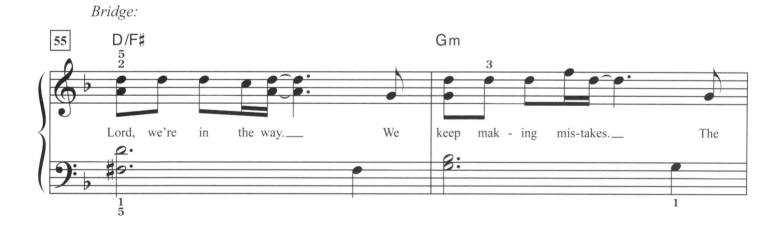

Bridge:

Lord, we're in the way.___ We keep mak-ing mis-takes.___ The

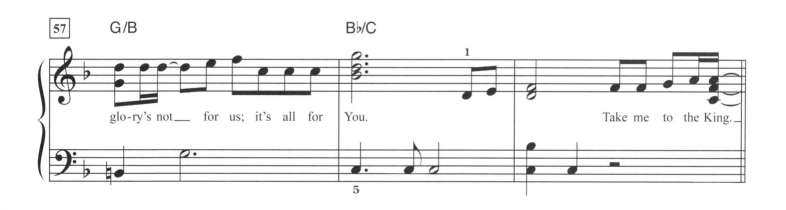

glo-ry's not___ for us; it's all for You. Take me to the King.

Chorus:

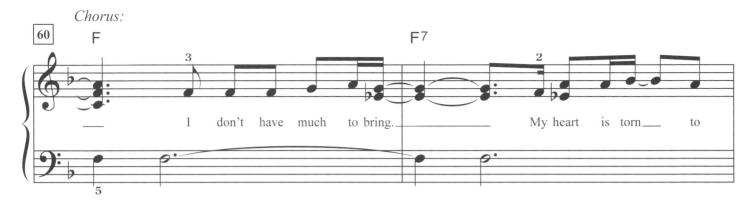

I don't have much to bring.___ My heart is torn___ to

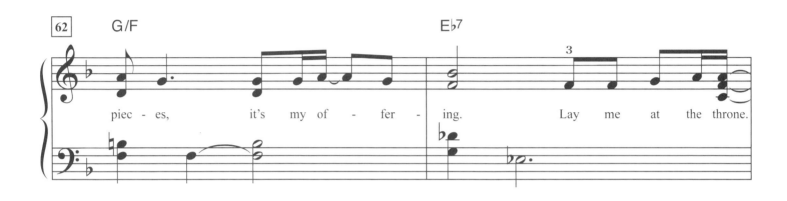

piec - es, it's my of - fer - ing. Lay me at the throne.

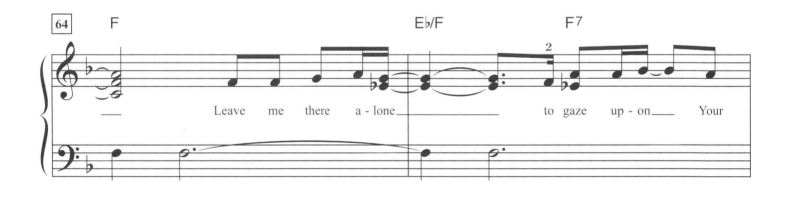

Leave me there a - lone___ to gaze up - on___ Your

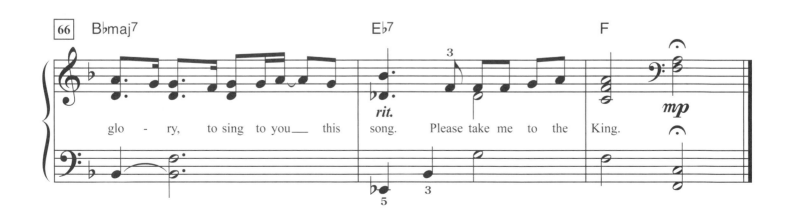

glo - ry, to sing to you___ this song. Please take me to the King.

Who You Are

Words and Music by Jason Walker,
Michael Gomez, Chad Mattson and Jon Lowry
Arr. Carol Tornquist

Bridge:

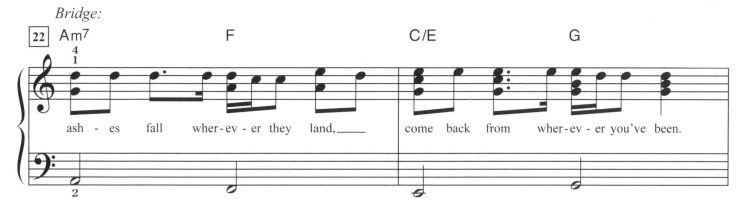

ash - es fall wher-ev - er they land,____ come back from wher-ev - er you've been.

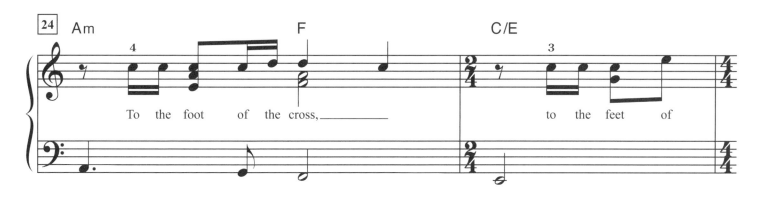

To the foot of the cross,____ to the feet of

Je - sus,____ the feet of Je - sus. You can nev - er fall

D.S. al Coda

Coda

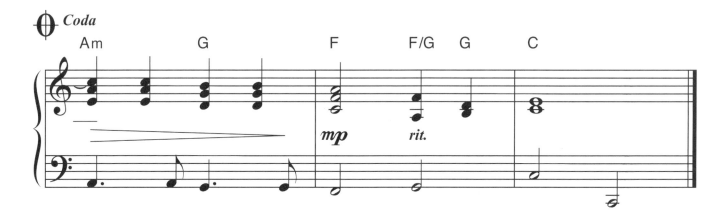

Verse 2:
You believe in freedom, but you don't know how to choose.
You gotta step out of your feelings that you're so afraid to lose.
And ev'ry day you put your feet on the floor, you gotta walk through the door.
It's never gonna be easy, but it's all worth fighting for.
(To Chorus:)

We Are

Words and Music by Ed Cash, Chuck Butler,
James Tealy and Hillary McBride
Arr. Carol Tornquist

Moderate rock, half-time feel

Verse:

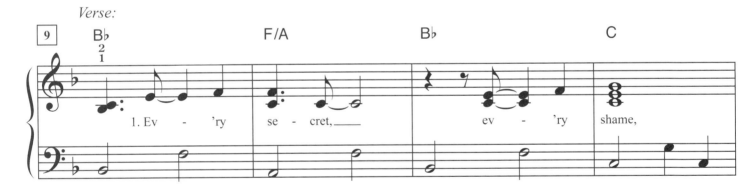

1. Ev-'ry se-cret,___ ev-'ry shame,

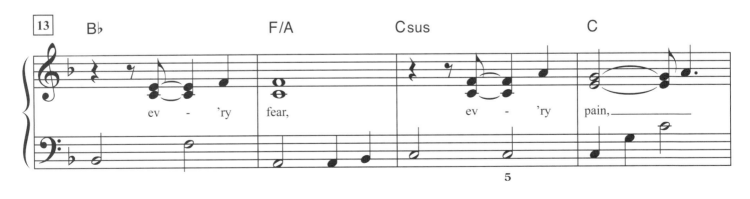

ev-'ry fear, ev-'ry pain,___

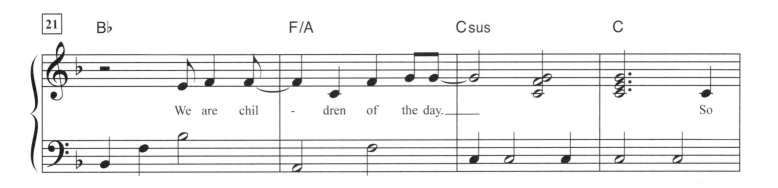

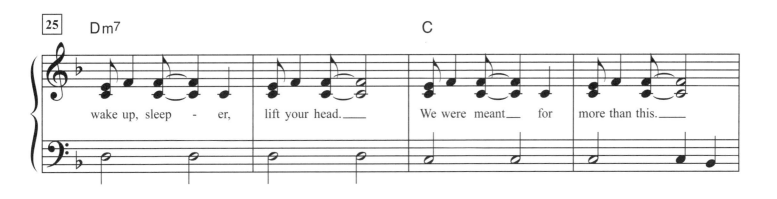

Chorus:

We are the light of the world._ We are the cit-y on a hill.__

We are the light of the world, and we got - ta, we got - ta, we got - ta let the light shine.

We are the light of the world._ We are the cit-y on the hill.__

We are the light of the world, and we got - ta, we got - ta, we got - ta let the light shine._

Whom Shall I Fear

(God of Angel Armies)

Words and Music by Chris Tomlin,
Ed Cash and Scott Cash
Arr. Carol Tornquist

You Are

Words and Music by Rhyan Shirley,
Jared Martin, Colton Dixon and Mike Busbee
Arr. Carol Tornquist

Chorus:

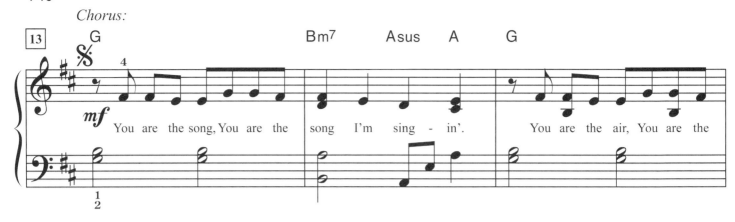

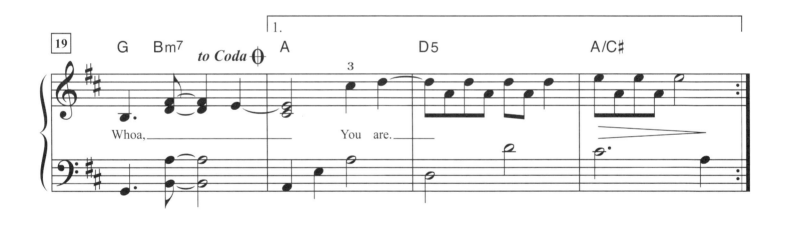

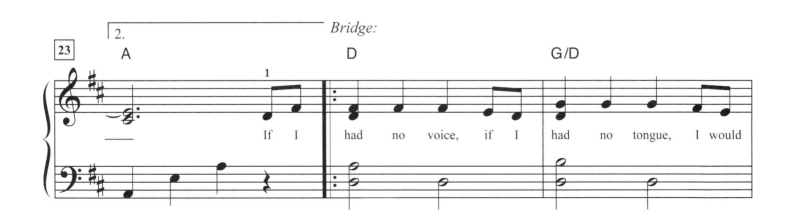

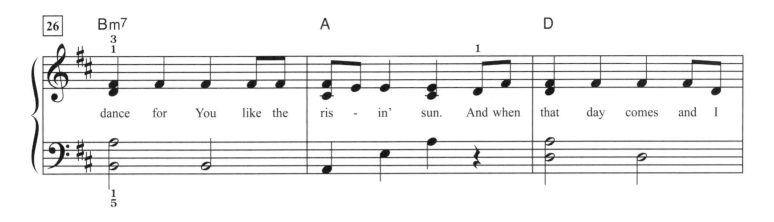

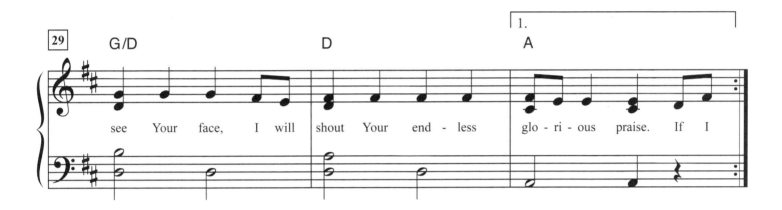

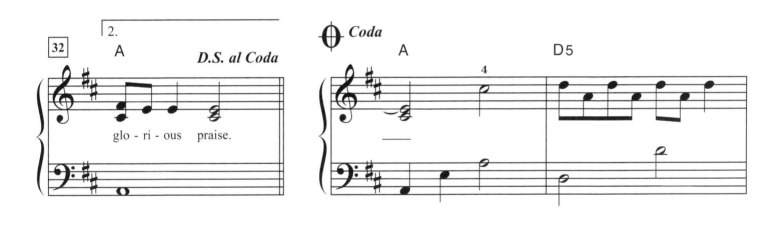

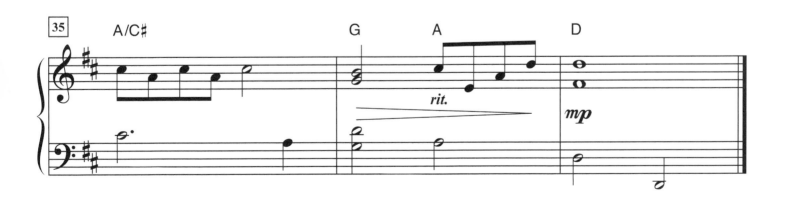

You Raise Me Up

Words and Music by
Rolf Lovland and Brendan Graham
Arr. Carol Tornquist

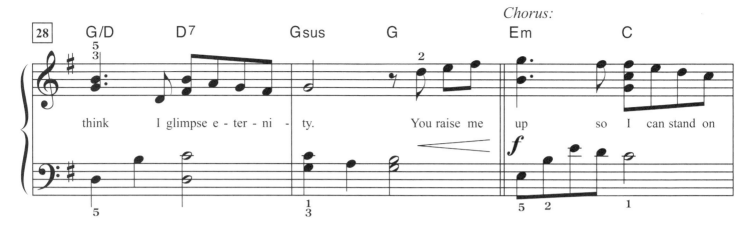

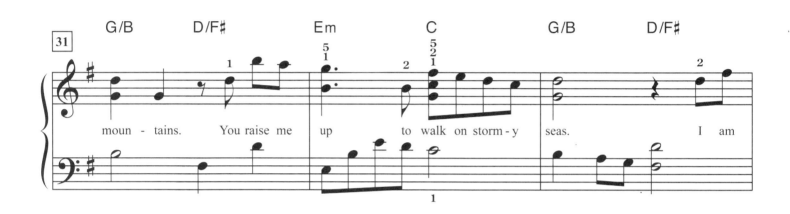

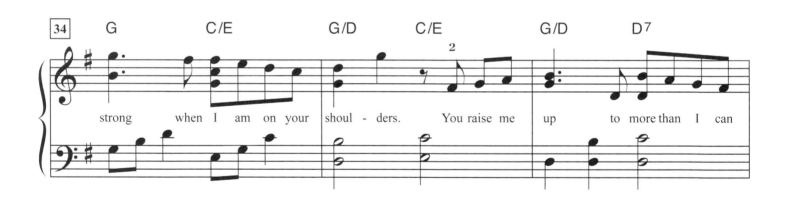

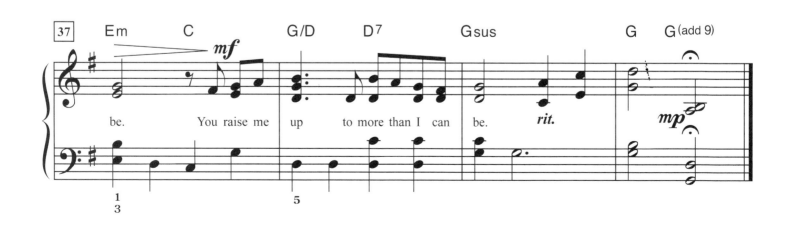

Your Love Never Fails

Words and Music by
Anthony Skinner and Chris McClarney
Arr. Carol Tornquist

Verse 2:
The wind is strong and the water's deep, but I'm not alone here in these open seas,
'Cause Your love never fails.
The chasm is far too wide; I never thought I'd reach the other side.
Your love never fails, oh no, oh no.
(To Chorus:)